Presidents

ANDREW JACKSON

A MyReportLinks.com Book

Stephen Feinstein

MyReportLinks.com Books

an imprint of

 Enslow Publishers, Inc.

Box 398, 40 Industrial Road
Berkeley Heights, NJ 07922
USA

MyReportLinks.com Books, an imprint of Enslow Publishers, Inc.

Library of Congress Cataloging-in-Publication Data

Feinstein, Stephen.
Andrew Jackson: A MyReportLinks.com Book / Stephen Feinstein.
     p. cm. — (Presidents)
   Includes bibliographical references (p.) and index.
   Summary: Traces the private and public life of America's seventh president, who
was orphaned at the age of fourteen. Includes Internet links to Web sites, source
documents, and photographs related to Andrew Jackson.
   ISBN 0-7660-5003-3
   1. Jackson, Andrew, 1767–1845—Juvenile literature. 2. Presidents—United
States—Biography—Juvenile literature. [1. Jackson, Andrew, 1767–1845.
2. Presidents.] 1. Title. II. Series.
E382 .F45 2002
973.5'6'092—dc21
[B]   2001004298

Printed in the United States of America

10 9 8 7 6 5 4 3 2 1

To Our Readers: We have done our best to make sure all Internet addresses in this book
were active and appropriate when we went to press. However, the author and the Publisher
have no control over, and assume no liability for, the material available on those Internet
sites or on other Web sites they may link to. The Publisher will try to keep the Report Links
that back up this book up to date on our Web site for three years from the book's
first publication date. Any comments or suggestions can be sent by e-mail to
comments@myreportlinks.com or to the address on the back cover.

Photo Credits: © Corel Corporation, pp. 1 (background), 3; Courtesy of
America's Library, The Library of Congress, pp. 26, 28; Courtesy of *American
History: The Magazine of the American Experience*, p. 35; Courtesy of
MyReportLinks.com Books, p. 4; Courtesy of The Florida Department of State,
Division of Historical Resources, p. 29; Courtesy of The Smithsonian Institution,
the National Museum of American History, p. 13; Courtesy of The University of
Virginia, p. 32; Courtesy of WGBH/PBS Online: Africans in America, p. 37; The
Hermitage: Home of President Andrew Jackson, Nashville, TN, pp. 1, 20, 30, 38,
44; The Library of Congress, pp. 22, 31, 41; The National Archives, p. 16.

Cover Photo: © Corel Corporation; The Hermitage: Home of President
Andrew Jackson, Nashville, TN.

Contents

		STOP						
Back	Forward	Stop	Review	Home	Explore	Favorites	History

About MyReportLinks.com Books

MyReportLinks.com Books
Great Books, Great Links, Great for Research!

MyReportLinks.com Books present the information you need to learn about your report subject. In addition, they show you where to go on the Internet for more information. The pre-evaluated Report Links, listed on **www.myreportlinks.com**, save hours of research time and link to dozens—even hundreds—of Web sites, source documents, and photos related to your report topic.

To Our Readers:
Each Report Link has been reviewed by our editors, who will work hard to keep only active and appropriate Internet addresses in our books and up to date on our Web site. However, the author and the Publisher have no control over, and assume no liability for, the material available on those Internet sites, or on other Web sites they may link to.

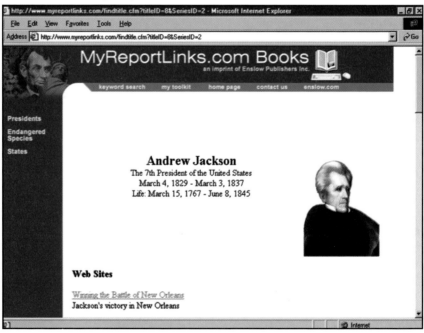

Access:
The Publisher will try to keep the Report Links that back up this book up to date on our Web site for three years from the book's first publication date. Please enter **PJA114C** if asked for a password.

Report Links

The Internet sites described below can be accessed at
http://www.myreportlinks.com

▶ **Winning the Battle of New Orleans**　　　　*EDITOR'S CHOICE*

America's Library is a Library of Congress Web site designed
specifically for young adults. This page describes Jackson's victory in
New Orleans. There are links to events and individuals from that time
period and others.

Link to this Internet site from http://www.myreportlinks.com

EDITOR'S CHOICE

▶ **A Brief Biography of Andrew Jackson, 1767–1845**

This biography of Jackson is simply written and easy to understand.
The profile chronicles Jackson's rise from poverty to the highest office
in the land.

Link to this Internet site from http://www.myreportlinks.com

EDITOR'S CHOICE

▶ **Duels and Dueling on the Web**

Growing up in the wilderness of Tennessee, Jackson lived by the
"frontier code of honor." That included challenging an attacker to a
duel. Here you will learn the facts of Jackson's famous duel with
Charles Dickinson and find links to other Jackson duels.

Link to this Internet site from http://www.myreportlinks.com

EDITOR'S CHOICE

▶ **LIBERTY! The American Revolution**

The Revolutionary War deeply affected young Andrew Jackson. This
site, from PBS, discusses how the colonies gained independence from
Britain and what liberty and freedom mean today.

Link to this Internet site from http://www.myreportlinks.com

EDITOR'S CHOICE

▶ **The Hermitage**

A visit to this site, the official home of Andrew Jackson's beloved
Hermitage, near Nashville, brings alive the excitement surrounding
Jackson's first run for the presidency. You can also take a virtual tour of
the estate and learn what life was like in the early nineteenth century.

Link to this Internet site from http://www.myreportlinks.com

EDITOR'S CHOICE

▶ **Andrew Jackson**

This site, part of the Internet Public Library's POTUS (Presidents of
the United States) series, provides an excellent quick-reference guide to
the life of Andrew Jackson. You will also find a list of his cabinet
members and the notable events of his presidency.

Link to this Internet site from http://www.myreportlinks.com

Report Links

➤ The Internet sites described below can be accessed at
http://www.myreportlinks.com

▶**Andrew Jackson: "Champion of the Kingly Commons"**
Born into poverty, Andrew Jackson rose to the highest office in the land,
largely due to his reputation as a military hero. This site explores how Jackson
acquired an image that was truly larger than life.

Link to this Internet site from http://www.myreportlinks.com

▶**Andrew Jackson's First Inaugural Address**
The text of Andrew Jackson's first and second inaugural addresses comes from
Bartleby.com's vast electronic library. Learn about Jackson's goals and
ambitions for the country that he was chosen to lead. Also provided are links
to more biographical information about Jackson.

Link to this Internet site from http://www.myreportlinks.com

▶**Andrew Jackson's Hermitage**
Andrew Jackson always believed in slavery and had many slaves while living at
the Hermitage. Although there is a wealth of information about Jackson,
information about his slaves is scarce. Join archaeologist Larry McKee as he
tries to uncover the truth about slavery at the Hermitage.

Link to this Internet site from http://www.myreportlinks.com

▶**The American President: Andrew Jackson**
The American Presidents series offers both quick reference and in-depth study
of Andrew Jackson. It provides a good starting point for research on Jackson.

Link to this Internet site from http://www.myreportlinks.com

▶**The American Presidency: Andrew Jackson**
Grolier's Multimedia American Presidency series offers both a quick-reference
guide to Andrew Jackson's life as well as a more comprehensive biography.

Link to this Internet site from http://www.myreportlinks.com

▶**Andrew Jackson, Seventh President, 1829–1837**
This White House profile of Andrew Jackson tells us that the former military
hero was very much a man of the people. From his inaugural party to his
"Kitchen Cabinet," Jackson wanted to include as many citizens as possible in
the United States government.

Link to this Internet site from http://www.myreportlinks.com

Report Links

The Internet sites described below can be accessed at http://www.myreportlinks.com

▶**Andrew Jackson's State of the Union Address**
In his State of the Union Address given on December 6, 1830, Andrew Jackson speaks of his visions for the Republic and the removal of Americans Indians from their homelands.

Link to this Internet site from http://www.myreportlinks.com

▶**Andrew Jackson and the Tavern-Keeper's Daughter**
One of the first major problems Jackson faced in office was the so-called "Petticoat Affair," which involved the wife of Secretary of War John Eaton. This site describes the scandal and the role of the press in fueling it.

Link to this Internet site from http://www.myreportlinks.com

▶**Andrew Jackson (1767–1845)**
Interlink Cafe contains Andrew Jackson's inaugural addresses and annual messages to Congress for his first and second terms as president. You will also find links to a biography of Jackson, his cabinet, and Jackson's farewell address.

Link to this Internet site from http://www.myreportlinks.com

▶**Andrew Jackson (1767–1845)**
By navigating through this site you will learn that among his several firsts, Andrew Jackson became the first American president to face an assassination attempt, on January 30, 1835.

Link to this Internet site from http://www.myreportlinks.com

▶**Bank of the United States**
One of Jackson's primary goals as president was to destroy the Bank of the United States. As a president of the people, Jackson felt that the bank was unconstitutional and hurt the poor. This site describes Jackson's battles with Congress over the bank.

Link to this Internet site from http://www.myreportlinks.com

▶**The Battle of New Orleans**
As the War of 1812 drew to a close, New Orleans was still in danger of being captured by the British. In January 1815, Andrew Jackson led an attack and won a total victory over the invading British fleet. This site describes the battle, preparations for it, and the key players involved.

Link to this Internet site from http://www.myreportlinks.com

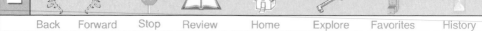
 The Internet sites described below can be accessed at
http://www.myreportlinks.com

▶**The Cherokee Trail of Tears**
As president, Andrew Jackson supported the forced removal of the Cherokee from their traditional homelands in the southern highlands. This site describes this sad chapter in American history with stories from survivors, a time line, and links to more information about those who died on the journey.

Link to this Internet site from http://www.myreportlinks.com

▶**Discovery School's A-to-Z History: Jackson, Andrew**
This site offers a comprehensive profile of Andrew Jackson and his journey from a childhood of poverty to two terms in the White House. You will also learn about Jackson's success as a military leader and how he received the nickname "Old Hickory."

Link to this Internet site from http://www.myreportlinks.com

▶**Encyclopedia Britannica Intermediate: Andrew Jackson**
Encyclopedia Britannica provides a comprehensive biography of our seventh president, Andrew Jackson. Here you will read everything from his early life to retirement and how he shaped the Democratic Party.

Link to this Internet site from http://www.myreportlinks.com

▶**TheHistoryNet: Old Hickory and the Pirate**
A statue of Andrew Jackson dominates Jackson Square in New Orleans, the city he kept out of British hands. This essay from *Historic Traveler* magazine tells of Jackson's unlikely collaboration with the pirate Jean Lafitte.

Link to this Internet site from http://www.myreportlinks.com

▶**Judgment Day: Indian Removal**
Conflict arose when white men expanded their settlements into the southern highlands occupied by American Indians. Andrew Jackson favored the expulsion of native people from their homelands to new homes in the West, a feat he eventually accomplished.

Link to this Internet site from http://www.myreportlinks.com

▶**Museum of the Waxhaws and Andrew Jackson Memorial**
Although most historians believe Andrew Jackson was actually born in nearby South Carolina, North Carolina continues to look upon Jackson as a native son. This museum in Waxhaw, North Carolina, celebrates Jackson's boyhood in the region and the American Indians who also lived there.

Link to this Internet site from http://www.myreportlinks.com

Report Links

The Internet sites described below can be accessed at http://www.myreportlinks.com

▶ **North Carolina Encyclopedia: Andrew Jackson**

So popular was Andrew Jackson that both North Carolina and South Carolina claim him as a native son. This North Carolina Encyclopedia entry chronicles Jackson's life from his birth in the Waxhaws border area to his two-term presidency.

Link to this Internet site from http://www.myreportlinks.com

▶ **Northern Georgia Creek History**

The Creek Indians controlled much of Georgia before settlers arrived in the New World. When the white colonists began to intrude on Creek land, the Creek were forced to declare war. This site explores the Creek way of life as well as battles fought against Andrew Jackson.

Link to this Internet site from http://www.myreportlinks.com

▶ **The Papers of Andrew Jackson**

The Avalon Project of the Yale Law School contains a large amount of primary source material on Andrew Jackson's presidency, including Jackson's speeches, proclamations, and letters. Readers can gain insight into Jackson's political philosophy.

Link to this Internet site from http://www.myreportlinks.com

▶ **Re-living History: The War of 1812**

This Web site provides an in-depth look at the War of 1812. It allows you to navigate through the causes, time lines, people, and the aftermath of the war. You can also view maps and battle diagrams.

Link to this Internet site from http://www.myreportlinks.com

▶ **The Seminole Wars**

This site, maintained by the Division of Historical Resources of the Florida Department of State, provides a brief overview of the three wars the United States waged against the Seminole. Andrew Jackson commanded American troops in the First Seminole War, in 1818.

Link to this Internet site from http://www.myreportlinks.com

▶ **The White House: Rachel Donelson Jackson**

Visit this White House site to learn more about Rachel Donelson Jackson, the wife of Andrew Jackson. Like her husband, Rachel was raised on the frontier, moving from Virginia to the Tennessee wilderness at the age of twelve.

Link to this Internet site from http://www.myreportlinks.com

Highlights

1767—*Mar. 15:* Born in Waxhaw County, South Carolina. Historians dispute the exact location.

1781—Jackson's mother, Elizabeth, dies, leaving him orphaned. His father had died before Andrew's birth.

Jackson and his brother Robert are taken prisoner by the British during the Revolutionary War.

1791—*Aug.:* Marries Mrs. Rachel Donelson Robards.

1794—*Jan. 18:* Remarries Rachel Donelson Robards after it is learned that the divorce from her first husband was never finalized.

1796—Elected as state of Tennessee's first congressman in the House of Representatives.

1797—Becomes U.S. senator from the state of Tennessee.

1798—Elected as a justice on the Tennessee Superior Court.

1806—Kills Charles Dickinson, a lawyer, in a duel, after Dickinson makes derogatory comments regarding Jackson's wife, Rachel.

1814—*Mar.:* Defeats Creek Indians led by Chief Red Eagle at the Battle of Horseshoe Bend.

1815—*Jan. 8:* Defeats the British in the Battle of New Orleans.

1818—Invades Florida and crushes Seminole Indians in what came to be known as the First Seminole War.

1821—Serves as military governor of Florida.

1823—Again elected to U.S. Senate.

1828—Elected as seventh president of the United States, beating the incumbent, John Quincy Adams.

1832—Reelected president, defeating Henry Clay. Vetoes the recharter of the Second Bank of the United States.

1835—*Jan. 30:* Richard Lawrence unsuccessfully attempts to assassinate President Jackson.

1845—*June 8:* Dies at his home, the Hermitage, in Nashville, Tennessee.

Code of Honor

When his mother died during the Revolutionary War, fourteen-year-old Andrew Jackson was left all alone in the world. Mrs. Elizabeth Jackson had gone off to Charleston, South Carolina, to nurse American soldiers who were being held on British prison ships. There the brave woman caught a fever and died. For the rest of his life, Jackson would always remember his mother's parting words as she left for Charleston. "You will have to make your own way. None will respect you more than you respect yourself . . . Avoid quarrels . . . but sustain your manhood always."[1] She would also tell him, "Andy . . . never tell a lie, nor take what is not your own, nor sue . . . for slander . . . settle them cases yourself."[2]

Jackson took his mother's words to heart, and he grew up to be a man known for his honesty, courage, and inclination to "settle them cases" by himself. In the sparsely settled frontier country of Tennessee, which would become Jackson's home, men were honor bound to settle disputes by participating in duels. Men who lived by this frontier code of honor typically relied on their skill with a gun to respond to any wrongs done to them, rather than seek legal solutions. During his long life, Jackson would never shrink from a fight. It is believed that he engaged in at least six, and possibly as many as one hundred, duels. He sustained serious wounds in two of them.

There was only one duel in which Jackson killed his opponent. In May 1806, Jackson challenged Charles Dickinson, a young lawyer, to a duel. Dickinson was

known to be an excellent shot, possibly the best in all Tennessee. He had on more than one occasion made insulting remarks about Jackson's wife, Rachel. There was also a misunderstanding about a horse race involving Jackson's horse Truxton. Jackson and Dickinson traded insults, each accusing the other of being a coward and a scoundrel. Finally, the duel was set for May 30, to take place at Harrison's Mills, Kentucky.

Early in the morning of May 30, Jackson and Dickinson, each accompanied by a small party of supporters, gathered on the Kentucky shore of the Red River. The two duelists faced each other at a distance of twenty-four feet. The pistols in their hands were pointed downward. Jackson had decided that he would allow Dickinson to fire the first shot. Then Jackson would take his time and kill Dickinson with a carefully aimed shot. At the signal to fire, Dickinson immediately fired his pistol. To his amazement, Jackson was still standing. Dickinson could hardly believe that his bullet had missed Jackson.

Had the two duelists not stood so far apart, Dickinson would probably have noticed the grimace of pain on Jackson's face as Jackson's left hand clutched his chest. Now it was Jackson's turn. He raised his pistol, took aim, and fired. Dickinson fell to the ground, the bullet having torn through his body, just below the ribs.

Later that night, before Dickinson died, he was told that Jackson had been seriously wounded and was dying. Only the first part was true. As they walked away from the riverbank, Jackson's friends noticed that Jackson's shoe was filled with blood. When asked if he had been hit, Jackson replied, "Oh, I believe he pinked me."[3] Then he added, "I'd have hit him if he'd shot me through the brain!"[4]

Later that day, Jackson learned that the bullet fired by Dickinson had shattered two of his ribs and lodged close to his heart. The man who would become the seventh president of the United States would carry that bullet in his body for the rest of his days. It served as a constant reminder of the high cost of living by the frontier code of honor.

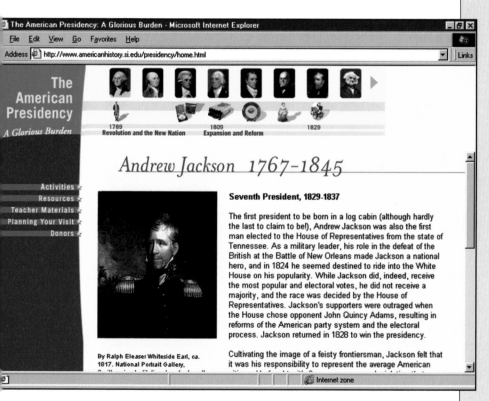

▲ This 1817 portrait of Andrew Jackson depicts him as a military hero.

Chapter 2 ▶

Early Years, 1767–1788

Andrew Jackson was born on March 15, 1767, in the family's cabin in the Waxhaw region, an area that straddled the border between North and South Carolina. He was the youngest of the three sons of Andrew and Elizabeth Jackson. Scots-Irish immigrants from the north of Ireland, Andrew and Elizabeth had arrived in the American colonies in 1765. They settled in the Waxhaw region, where several of Elizabeth's married sisters already lived.

▶ A Father He Never Knew

Hoping to escape a life of poverty in Ireland, the Jacksons found a different life of hardship and poverty in the Carolinas. Andrew's father built a cabin, cleared the land, and planted crops to feed his family. But the struggle to build a new life in the wilderness was as dangerous as it was exhausting. Just a few weeks before Andrew was born, Mr. Jackson injured himself lifting a log and died a few hours later.

In order to provide for Andrew and his brothers, Andrew's mother moved in with her sister, Jane Crawford, and Jane's husband, William. The Crawfords had established a successful farm in nearby Lancaster County, South Carolina. They owned slaves, who did most of the fieldwork. Elizabeth worked as a housekeeper for the Crawfords. Andrew Jackson grew to young manhood on the Crawford farm and the surrounding land.

▶ Tough Youngster

Andrew was a wild young boy who was not afraid of anyone or anything. He was constantly getting into fights with the neighbor boys. He often fought with those bigger and older than himself.

When Andrew was old enough for school, Elizabeth sent him to a Presbyterian academy at Waxhaw Church. Andrew learned to read by the age of five and to write by age eight. He also learned how to keep accounts.

One of Andrew's favorite activities was racing—on foot or on horseback. With Andrew, winning was everything. He loved competition and never gave up. On the rare occasion that he was beaten, he would never forgive or forget his opponent.

▶ A New Nation

In 1776, when Andrew was nine years old, delegates to the Second Continental Congress in Philadelphia signed the Declaration of Independence. Since many of Andrew's neighbors could neither read nor write, Andrew would often serve as a public reader, reading the newspaper aloud to them. In mid-July 1776, Andrew stood before a gathering of thirty to forty of his neighbors and read aloud the words of the new Declaration of Independence.

The Revolutionary War, which had been raging in the North, reached the back country of South Carolina as Andrew reached his teens. The Revolution brought terrible tragedy to the young man. For years, his mother, Elizabeth, had told her sons tales of Irish heroes fighting British tyranny. Now the British were the enemy once again. In 1779, Andrew's oldest brother, Hugh, then eighteen, enlisted in a militia regiment. Hugh died at the Battle of Stone Ferry, where Americans drove the British back into Georgia.

By May 1780, Charleston had fallen to the British, and British troops were sent into the Carolina back country. In Lancaster County, the fighting took place not only between the American troops and the British troops but also between the citizens themselves. The Whigs were mainly poor Irish settlers, like the Jacksons, who opposed British rule. The Tories were mostly Scottish colonists loyal to the British crown. In a battle in Jackson's Waxhaw region, the British killed more than a hundred American militiamen, slaughtering many after they had surrendered. Wounded survivors of the massacre took refuge at Waxhaw Church. Elizabeth and her two remaining sons, sixteen-year-old Robert and thirteen-year-old Andrew, went to the church to help care for the wounded.

▲ In May of 1780, at the Battle of Camden, in South Carolina, the British troops forced the Americans to retreat. The Revolutionary War had entered the Carolina back country, and thirteen-year-old Andrew Jackson would soon be involved. He and his brother enlsted in a cavalry where Andrew served as a messsenger.

Joining the Continental Army

When Andrew learned more of the gruesome details of the massacre, he burned with rage against the British. He was reported to have said, "Oh, if I were a man, how I would sweep down the British with my grass blade."[1] Soon afterward, Andrew and his brother Robert enlisted in Colonel William R. Davie's Whig cavalry. Andrew was thoroughly familiar with the surrounding country, so he served as a mounted messenger. In recognition of Andrew's good work, the colonel gave him a pistol.

On April 10, 1781, Andrew and Robert were seeking to avoid capture by the British. They took refuge in their cousin Thomas Crawford's house near Waxhaw. A Tory gave them away, and British troops barged into the house. When a British officer ordered Andrew to clean the officer's boots, the brave boy refused, declaring that he was a prisoner of war. The enraged officer slashed at Andrew with his sword. As Andrew raised his hand for protection, the sword cut through to the bone and caused severe injury to his head. Andrew's brother Robert was also struck with a sword.

Painful Experience

Dazed and bleeding, both boys were then taken to a prison stockade forty miles away in Camden, South Carolina. Conditions at the prison were dreadful. The boys received no medical attention, and their wounds became infected. They were denied adequate food and water. Then they caught smallpox. Two weeks later, Elizabeth arrived in Camden to rescue her sons. She persuaded the prison commander to include them in a prisoner exchange that had been arranged. She then brought her sons home, but

Robert died two days later. Andrew gradually recovered, but it took him several months.

That summer, when Andrew was once again healthy, Elizabeth left for Charleston to care for other American prisoners of war. The fighting ended shortly thereafter, with the British surrender at Yorktown, Virginia, in October 1781. Andrew never saw his mother again. In November 1781, he was notified that Elizabeth had died from cholera.

▶ Finding His Own Way

At the age of fourteen, Andrew was orphaned. He lived briefly with various relatives. One of the relatives, Joseph White, owned a saddle shop in which Andrew worked for a while. At sixteen, he got a job teaching school, but within a year he grew bored. He then decided he wanted to become a lawyer. In 1784, he moved to Salisbury, North Carolina, where he studied law for two years under Spruce McCay, a successful local attorney. After that, he worked for six months in the law office of John Stokes.

In September 1787, Jackson was admitted to the North Carolina bar, the state's association of lawyers and other legal professionals. Early the following year, he and a group of lawyer friends, including John McNairy, traveled westward on horseback into the wilderness to seek fame and fortune. In Jonesboro, in what would become the eastern part of the state of Tennessee, Jackson and McNairy interrupted their journey. For several months they remained in Jonesboro, where Jackson handled several law cases. On September 25, 1788, the wilderness beckoned once again. Jackson and McNairy joined a caravan of sixty families traveling west across the Cumberland Mountains to the frontier settlement at Nashville.

Frontier Hero, 1788–1828

Although the 183-mile-long trail from Jonesboro to Nashville was dangerous, Jackson and the other travelers reached Nashville safely on October 26, 1788. However, some hunters who had stayed at one of the Jackson caravan's campsites were killed, while they slept, by the Cherokee.

▶ A Move to Nashville

Nashville in 1788 was not much more than a raw settlement in the wilderness. It had been founded just nine years earlier by Colonel John Donelson and James Robertson. As Jackson rode into town, he saw only a cluster of cabins and tents, a couple of stores and taverns, and a log courthouse. A variety of wagons stood in the street, and horses were hitched to posts. Buffalo grazed on the lands right outside the settlement.

On November 3, 1788, John McNairy took office as judge for what was then the western district of North Carolina (later to become part of Tennessee). McNairy appointed Jackson to serve as public prosecutor. One of the main legal problems involved people who refused to pay their debts to local merchants. Business in Nashville had practically come to a halt. In a single day, the energetic Jackson issued seventy court orders to debtors on behalf of the merchants. Suddenly business revived as law and order arrived in the wilderness—in the person of Andrew Jackson.

Respected Lawyer

Before long, Jackson had more work than he could handle. Anyone in the area with a legal problem came knocking on his door. Most cases involved sales, land disputes, debts, and assault and battery. Since there was little money in circulation in the wilderness, Jackson was often paid for his legal services with farm produce, animals, slaves, and land. The land, however, still legally belonged to the Cherokee.

Jackson had taken up lodgings at the Donelson stockade, about ten miles outside Nashville. He preferred this to the Red Heifer Tavern near the courthouse. Mrs. Donelson, the widow of Colonel John Donelson (who had been killed several years earlier on a surveying trip), rented out small cabins at the stockade, and provided meals in the main house. Jackson shared a cabin with another young lawyer named John Overton, who had recently arrived from Kentucky. The two quickly became friends, and remained so throughout their lives. The two men set up a law practice in their cabin.

Jackson Meets Rachel Donelson

While living at the Donelson stockade, Jackson became attracted to Mrs. Donelson's beautiful twenty-one-year-old daughter, Rachel. There

Andrew Jackson met, and fell in love with, Rachel Donelson Robards while he was living at the Donelson Stockade, ten miles outside of Nashville.

Tools   Search   Notes   Discuss   Go!

was only one problem—Rachel was already married. Rachel Donelson had married Lewis Robards at the age of seventeen. The marriage was a disaster from the start, and they separated. When Robards pleaded with Rachel to give their marriage another chance, she reluctantly agreed. Then, when Robards learned about Jackson, he accused Rachel of being unfaithful and threatened to kill Jackson. Proclaiming his innocence, Jackson challenged Robards to a duel, but was turned down.

Rachel went off to live with Robards in Kentucky, but the two soon began quarreling again. Mrs. Donelson begged Jackson to bring her daughter Rachel back from Kentucky. When Jackson did so, Robards accused his wife of eloping with Jackson. Robards then traveled to Nashville to make a final attempt at reconciliation with his wife, letting people know that Jackson's behavior toward Rachel was inappropriate. Robards's accusations angered Jackson. A furious Jackson went looking for Robards and told him, "If you ever again associate my name with your wife's, I'll cut off your ears—I'm tempted to do it anyhow."[1] At this point, Robards wisely decided to quit while he still had his ears.

Marriage and Remarriage

By this time, Jackson had indeed fallen in love with Rachel, and she with him. In 1791, Rachel divorced Robards and married Jackson. That same year, Jackson was appointed attorney general by the territorial governor of Tennessee.

Two years later, Jackson and Rachel received the shocking news that their marriage was invalid because her divorce from Robards had never been finalized. In January 1794, Jackson and Rachel got married all over again. Still, the fact that Rachel had been married to two men at the same time would be used in the future by Jackson's political enemies to attack both his character and Rachel's

On June 4, 1796, Tennessee was admitted to the Union as the sixteenth state. Jackson was a delegate to the convention in Knoxville that drafted the Tennessee Constitution. By this time he was one of the wealthiest men in the state of Tennessee. He had been speculating in land and slaves, and now he owned huge tracts of land. He built a 650-acre plantation, about twelve miles outside Nashville, that he called the Hermitage.

▶ Congressman Jackson

In the fall of 1796, near the end of President George Washington's second administration, Jackson was elected to represent Tennessee in the U.S. Congress in Philadelphia. Jackson shocked many congressmen when he voted against a statement praising Washington's accomplishments. Jackson, who throughout his life felt hatred toward Britain, believed that Washington's foreign policies favored the British too much.

In 1795, Jackson had been especially outraged when Washington signed the treaty negotiated between John Jay, chief justice of the United States, and the British. During Britain's war with France, the British had ignored America's neutrality and had seized American ships and forced American sailors to serve on British warships. From Jackson's perspective, Washington was so eager to improve relations with Britain that he caved in

In 1795, Andrew Jackson called for the impeachment of President George Washington over Washington's signing of the Jay Treaty. John Jay, pictured left, the first chief justice of the United States, had negotiated the treaty between the United States and Great Britain in 1794, after Britain had seized American ships and had ignored American neutrality.

to British demands. Jackson even declared that Washington should be impeached for signing the Jay Treaty because the Jay Treaty so overlooked the rights of Americans.

Jackson also criticized Washington's treaties with the American Indians. This won Jackson the support of white settlers in Tennessee. Throughout his political career, Jackson promoted the interests of white settlers at the expense of American Indians when it came to ownership of land.

Short Stint as Senator

In 1797, Jackson got into an argument with his old friend Judge John McNairy, and then with Tennessee governor John Sevier. Jackson challenged both of them to duels. Fortunately, neither of the duels was fought. That same year, Jackson was elected U.S. senator, but after serving just five months, he resigned, in April 1798. Apparently, Jackson was disappointed with the policies of President John Adams's administration. He also grew impatient with the slow pace of the legislative process. Jackson returned to Tennessee, where he was elected justice to the Tennessee Superior Court, a position he would hold until 1804.

Life at the Hermitage

In 1806, and in adherence to the frontier code of justice, Jackson killed the young lawyer Charles Dickinson in a duel after Dickinson questioned the honor of Jackson's beloved wife, Rachel. Jackson did much more than fight duels, though. He tended to his plantation, the Hermitage, and engaged in business ventures such as horse trading and river-boat construction. Because Jackson and Rachel were childless, Rachel grew lonely whenever Jackson was away from home. In 1810, Rachel and Andrew Jackson adopted one of the twin baby boys of Rachel's brother Severn Donelson. They

named the child Andrew, Jr. Another nephew, Andrew Jackson Donelson, came to live with them a few years later.

▶ War of 1812

By 1812, it had become clear to many Americans that another war with Britain was inevitable. Relations between the two nations had grown so bad that no other course seemed possible. Despite the signing of the Jay Treaty, the British continued to seize American ships on the high seas. They also armed the Indians in the western territories and encouraged them to attack white settlers. Finally, Congress declared war on Britain. Andrew Jackson again answered the call of his country.

Governor William Blount of Tennessee appointed Jackson major general of the U.S. Volunteers. Ordered to lead his 2,070 recruits south to repel an expected British invasion, Jackson marched his army over five hundred miles to Natchez, in the Mississippi Territory (present-day Mississippi and Alabama). The plan was to invade Spanish Florida and catch the British by surprise. By the time he reached Natchez, Jackson received new orders. The British invasion had been called off, and Jackson was ordered to demobilize his force.

An angry Jackson would do no such thing. He refused to leave his troops so far from home without supplies or support. Instead, he borrowed money for the barest minimum of supplies and led his troops back to Tennessee under severe conditions. They arrived home in May 1813. Because Jackson shared his men's hardships, they admired his courage and began calling him Old Hickory, because hickory wood is so tough.

During the summer of 1813, Jackson was ordered to attack the Creek Indians in the Mississippi Territory and put an end to an uprising there. Shawnee chief Tecumseh had encouraged the Creek to fight for their lands. He promised that the British would help them against the Americans. When war broke out between Britain and America, the Creek saw an opportunity to take back their lands.

On August 30, 1813, the Creek attacked Fort Mims, north of Mobile, in the Mississippi Territory (now Alabama), killing more than 250 soldiers and settlers. Jackson gathered a force of two thousand Tennessee volunteer militiamen and led them south.

▶ Battle of Horseshoe Bend

In November, Jackson's army defeated one thousand Creek at Talladega. Then, on March 27, 1814, Jackson's army attacked the Creek settlement at Horseshoe Bend, on the Tallapoosa River. More than five hundred Creek were killed during the battle. Hundreds more were killed trying to escape. In recognition of his military success, Jackson, on May 1, 1814, was promoted to the rank of major general in the U.S. Army.

On August 9, 1814, Jackson presented the Creek chief Red Eagle with a treaty that had truly harsh terms. The Creek had to give up claims to nearly twenty-three million acres of land—about one-fifth of Georgia and three-fifths of present-day Alabama. Chief Red Eagle realized that the Creek people would never be able to retake their lands. He had no choice but to sign the treaty, which ended the American Indian threat on the western frontier during the War of 1812.

Soon after, Jackson once again made plans to repel a British invasion. He marched his army down to Pensacola in Spanish Florida, and, believing the town belonged to the British, he attacked and captured the place. Then he learned that a fleet of British warships was waiting off the

coast of Cuba, preparing to attack the mainland. Assuming the British would land at Mobile, Jackson led his forces there. He soon learned that the British target was New Orleans. Jackson and his army scrambled to New Orleans, arriving there on December 2, 1814. Jackson immediately prepared for the attack.

Jackson enlisted the help of various groups to supplement his military force. Freed African-American slaves, Choctaw Indians, and the pirate Jean Laffite and his men joined Jackson's army. The combined forces dug defensive trenches in the swamps along the Mississippi River, a few miles east of the city.

▲ This portrait refers to "Major General Jackson," a rank Jackson attained after the Battle of Horseshoe Bend.

Battle of New Orleans

On the morning of January 8, 1815, the British launched their attack. Leading the British troops was Major General Sir Edward Pakenham, brother-in-law of the Duke of Wellington. The six thousand advancing British troops marched in columns sixty abreast. Jackson's men, although greatly outnumbered, waited patiently in their trenches until the British came within firing range. Then the Americans let loose one round after another of artillery and rifle fire. The British soldiers went down, row by row, cut to pieces by the American guns. More than two thousand British soldiers were either killed or wounded. Among the dead were General Pakenham and two other British generals. Amazingly, there were only fewer than one hundred American casualties. The Battle of New Orleans was over. Jackson's army had won a stunning victory. Unfortunately, no one knew that a peace treaty had been signed two weeks earlier.

On December 24, 1814, the United States and Britain had signed the peace treaty at Ghent, Belgium, officially ending the War of 1812. Among the American negotiators were Henry Clay and John Quincy Adams. Unfortunately, because news in those days traveled so slowly, neither Jackson nor anyone else in America knew that the war was over. Ironically, news of Jackson's victory reached Washington, D.C., on February 11, 1815, the same day word arrived of the signing of the Treaty of Ghent.

Though the Battle of New Orleans need never have been fought, Americans were thrilled by Jackson's victory. They were delighted to have a new hero. Congress awarded the "Hero of New Orleans" the Congressional Gold Medal, its highest honor. President Madison praised Jackson for achieving such a stunning victory with so few American casualties.

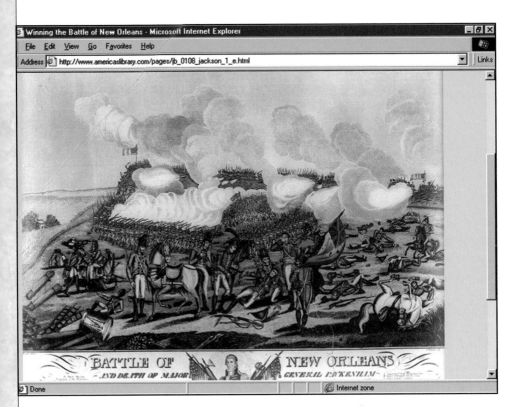

Winning the Battle of New Orleans - Microsoft Internet Explorer

File   Edit   View   Go   Favorites   Help

Address http://www.americaslibrary.com/pages/jb_0108_jackson_1_e.html   Links

BATTLE OF   NEW ORLEANS
AND DEATH OF MAJOR   GENERAL PAKENHAM

Done   Internet zone

This engraving depicts the Battle of New Orleans, in which Andrew Jackson's army was victorious. Unfortunately, a peace treaty had already been signed before the battle took place.

In 1818, Jackson was once again called upon to serve his country. President James Monroe was concerned that settlements in Georgia had come under attack by raiding bands of Seminole Indians from Spanish Florida. He wrote to Jackson, asking him to correct the situation. Jackson, assuming Monroe was authorizing an invasion of Spanish Florida, proceeded to launch one. After attacking Seminole villages and killing many of the people who lived there, Jackson's army once again captured Pensacola on May 24, 1818. Jackson threw out the Spanish governor and claimed the territory for the United States.

The Spanish were outraged and demanded that Jackson be punished. Many in Congress were prepared to satisfy the Spanish demand in order to keep the peace with Spain. U.S. Secretary of State John Quincy Adams strongly defended Jackson's actions as having been warranted by the situation in Spanish Florida. The following year, Spain agreed to transfer the territory of Spanish Florida to the United States under the terms of the Adams-Onís Treaty of 1819. In exchange for Florida, the United States agreed upon a border with Spanish land in the West, and assumed $5 million of legal claims that U.S. citizens had made against Spain. Two years later, in 1821, Jackson served as military governor of Florida for several months.

Seminole Wars - Microsoft Internet Explorer

File   Edit   View   Go   Favorites   Help

Address http://dhr.dos.state.fl.us/flafacts/semwar.html   Links

The First Seminole War

Back when Britain controlled Florida, the British often incited Seminoles against American settlers who were migrating south into Seminole territory. These old conflicts, combined with the safe-haven Seminoles provided black slaves, caused the U.S. army to attack the tribe in the First Seminole War (1817-1818), which took place in Florida and southern Georgia. Forces under Gen. Andrew Jackson quickly defeated the Seminoles.

St. Marks, Fla., April 1818 – Two Seminole chiefs, or *micos* are captured by Jackson's forces who used the ruse of flying the British flag to lure the Indians to them.

Picture from the Florida State Archives.

Finally, after several official and unofficial U.S. military expeditions into the territory, Spain formally ceded Florida to the United States in 1821, according to terms of the Adams-Onís Treaty.

As soon as the United States acquired Florida, it began urging the Indians there to leave their lands and relocate along with other southeastern tribes to Indian Territory, present-day Oklahoma

Done   Internet zone

Forces under General Andrew Jackson defeated the Seminole in Spanish Florida.

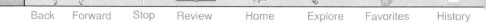

▲ This portrait captures Andrew Jackson as a Tennessee gentleman. It was painted shortly before he was elected president.

▶ Back to the Senate

In 1823, Jackson was once again elected U.S. senator by the Tennessee legislature. The following year, because of his immense popularity, he was persuaded by his political friends from Tennessee to run for president. Jackson at first refused, saying, "Do they think I am such a damned fool as to think myself fit for President of the United States?"[2] Jackson claimed that he was not so vain as to entertain such a notion, and he would make no effort to seek such an office. He did admit he would serve his country if called upon to do so.

When the Tennessee legislature nominated Jackson for president, the other presidential hopefuls criticized him. According to opponent John Quincy Adams, Jackson was "a barbarian who could not write a sentence of grammar and hardly could spell his own name."[3] Jackson's other opponents were William Crawford of Georgia and Henry Clay of Kentucky. John C. Calhoun of South Carolina dropped out early on, deciding to run for vice president instead.

▶ Bitter Loss

Jackson received the most popular votes as well as the most electoral votes. Yet, none of the candidates received a majority (at least 50 percent) of the electoral votes, so the House of Representatives got to choose the winner from among the three candidates who had received the highest number of electoral votes: Jackson with ninety-nine electoral votes, Adams with eighty-four, and Crawford with forty-one. Clay had only thirty-seven electoral votes and was forced out of the race. Because he was still Speaker of the House, Clay used his powerful influence in Congress to support Adams against Jackson. As a result, Adams became president. Calhoun was elected vice president, and Clay was appointed secretary of state.

Jackson's supporters were furious at the outcome of the election, believing that Adams had stolen the election from Jackson. Determined that Adams should be a one-term president, they immediately began working on the 1828 campaign to make sure that Jackson would be the next president. In 1825, Jackson resigned his Senate seat in order to put all of his energies into the presidential campaign.

All of the leading political figures were Republicans. But the Republicans were now split into two factions—the National Republicans and the Democratic-Republicans (later to be known as the Democrats). Adams was a National Republican, interested in federal programs that would benefit the nation as a whole. Jackson was a Democratic-Republican, a supporter of states' rights and programs that would benefit individual states or regions.

Speaker of the House Henry Clay played an important part in the presidential election of 1824, in which Andrew Jackson received the greatest number of popular votes among the candidates, but no candidate received a majority. Clay, who held considerable influence in Congress, supported John Quincy Adams over Jackson, and Adams became president. Clay's reward was to be appointed secretary of state.

Election of 1828

As the 1828 election approached, the campaign grew more heated. Bitter accusations flew back and forth. Newspaper editors frequently printed articles attacking the character of candidates they opposed. Jackson's enemies dredged up the circumstances of his marriage and remarriage to Rachel.

In November 1828, Jackson defeated Adams in a landslide victory. Jackson's triumph, though, was soon replaced by sorrow. On December 22, his beloved wife, Rachel, died of a heart attack. A grieving, bitter Jackson blamed her death on his opponents and their personal attacks on her honor, and that bitterness would affect his judgment as president.

The above image on the left portrays the realistic 'mob' that descended on the White House to celebrate Jackson's victory in 1828, while the image on the right is the idealized version of a 'civilized' inaugural ceremony -- now hanging in the capitol rotunda.

In a contest of personalities, Jackson had all the advantages. A strong military commander who valued the will of the people, he was also a charismatic and passionate man of action. Adams had government experience, but was formal and cold when speaking. His aristocratic demeanor and reputation for disdain of the masses did not aid in a competition against the popular Jackson. Jackson's position was clearly stated and the contrast noted as Jackson announced in his first inaugural address, "The majority is to govern."

▲ *Jackson's victory in the 1828 presidential election is pictured as both a wild celebration and a more sedate ceremony.*

Chapter 4 ▶ First Administration, 1829–1833

On March 4, 1829, thousands of people poured into Washington, D.C., to attend the inauguration of Andrew Jackson, the nation's seventh president. Among the excited throng were fur trappers and mountain men from the west, settlers and farmers, and common working people for whom Jackson was a hero.

▶ Inauguration Day

An informal reception was held at the White House after the inauguration ceremony. Perhaps as many as twenty thousand wildly cheering Jackson supporters tried to enter the White House, and a near riot ensued. In the confusion, an exhausted Jackson had to be whisked away through a side entrance for his own safety.

Shortly after becoming president, Jackson announced a policy of rotation for government officeholders. He replaced many government employees from the Adams administration with common people who had supported him. This method of rotating officeholders came to be known as the spoils system. Jackson justified this practice as necessary to give all citizens an equal opportunity to participate in self-government. Believing that officeholders should never feel that they or their children had a vested right to the office, he wrote, "It is rotation in office that will perpetuate our liberty."[1]

Kitchen Cabinet

In addition to Jackson's official cabinet, which included Martin Van Buren as secretary of state, there was an informal group of advisers consisting of western newspaper editors and politicians who had helped elect Jackson. This group became known as Jackson's Kitchen Cabinet, because they were said to slip into the White House through the rear entrance, and Jackson would meet with them in the kitchen.

A major challenge to President Jackson and the Union arose over the issue of protective tariffs. The federal government had levied a tax on imported manufactured goods in order to protect American manufacturers. In 1830, Vice President Calhoun backed South Carolina's protest against a high protective tariff. With few manufacturers, that state received little benefit from the protective tariff and had to pay higher prices for manufactured goods. To appease South Carolina, Congress in 1832 proposed a moderate reduction of the tariff. The congressmen from South Carolina were not satisfied. On November 24, 1832, South Carolina declared the tariffs of 1828 and 1832 to be null and void, and warned that it would prohibit enforcement of the tariff within its boundaries after February 1, 1833. Thus began a battle with Calhoun and South Carolina that would continue.

The Eaton Affair

But Jackson's relationship with Calhoun had begun to deteriorate earlier. And indeed, his relationship with his entire cabinet would suffer. In 1831, Peggy O'Neale Eaton, the wife of Secretary of War John H. Eaton, was snubbed by the wives of the other cabinet members. Vice

President Calhoun's wife led the attack on Mrs. Eaton. Jackson, still in mourning for his wife, and still insistent that the attacks on her had led to her death, defended Mrs. Eaton and considered the attacks on her character to be the work of his enemies. The result was that Secretary of War Eaton and Secretary of State Van Buren resigned, and soon after, the rest of the cabinet followed suit.

▷ Nullification

On December 28, 1832, Calhoun resigned the vice presidency in order to better serve his state of South Carolina in the Senate. Calhoun said that if the federal

Library of Congress

In 1831 President Andrew Jackson's defense of Mrs. Eaton led to the dissolution of his cabinet, a situation lampooned in this political cartoon.

▲ In this political cartoon of 1831, Jackson's defense of Mrs. Eaton is lampooned.

government did not allow a state to declare a law null and void, that state had the right to secede from the Union. Although Jackson was a believer in states' rights, he thought this exceeded the rights granted to the states under the Constitution. He threatened to send thousands of federal troops to South Carolina, if need be, to enforce the tariff laws and to keep the Union together. On March 2, 1833, South Carolina agreed to a Compromise Tariff proposed by Senator Henry Clay of Kentucky.

In contrast to his treatment of South Carolina, Jackson made no effort to prevent the state of Georgia from defying federal authority. In 1829, Georgia passed laws depriving the Cherokee people of their rights to own land (on which gold had recently been discovered) and to govern themselves. These laws violated previous treaties between the federal government and the American Indians. When the Cherokee protested to the federal government, Jackson's secretary of war, John H. Eaton, told them, "If you will go to the setting sun there you will be happy; there you can remain in peace and quietness; so long as waters run and the oaks grow that country shall be guaranteed to you and no white man shall be permitted to settle near you."[2]

▶ Indian Removal

Jackson supported congressional passage of the Indian Removal Act of 1830, by which American Indians in all of the twenty-four states were to be moved to lands west of the Mississippi River. Most of this Indian Territory would later become the state of Oklahoma. In his second Annual Message to Congress, in December 1830, Jackson said, "The waves of population and civilization are rolling to the westward, and we now propose to acquire the countries occupied by the red men of the South and West by a fair exchange . . ."[3] American

Indians were pressured into signing treaties legalizing their removal, typically granting them perpetual rights to lands of their own. These treaties were routinely broken once white settlement had begun to encroach on Indian lands. Then the Indians would face removal once again.

In 1831, Chief Justice John Marshall upheld the right of Georgia's Cherokee Nation to ignore that state's laws regarding the Indians. When Georgia refused to abide by the Supreme Court ruling, Jackson did nothing about it, thus paving the way for the shameful tragedy known as the Trail of Tears. Over the winter of 1838–39, Georgia's fifteen

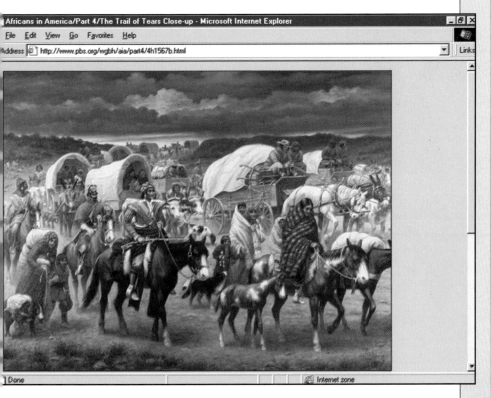

Africans in America/Part 4/The Trail of Tears Close-up - Microsoft Internet Explorer

File   Edit   View   Go   Favorites   Help

Address http://www.pbs.org/wgbh/aia/part4/4h1567b.html   Links

Done   Internet zone

▲ *The forced march west of the Cherokee during the winter of 1838–39 became known as the Trail of Tears. Nearly one quarter of them died before reaching the land that is today Oklahoma.*

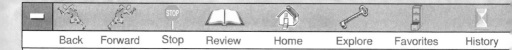
thousand Cherokee were removed from their lands and forced to march to the Indian Territory in what is now Oklahoma. About one quarter of them died along the way.

▶ Jackson Vetoes Bank Recharter

On July 10, 1832, Jackson vetoed a congressional bill to renew the charter of the Second Bank of the United States. To Jackson, the bank, under the direction of Nicholas Biddle, favored the interests of America's wealthiest and most powerful citizens at the expense of the common working people. This presidential veto led to a conflict over financial policy that would continue through Jackson's second term.

In the election of 1832, the presidential candidates were chosen by national political conventions for the first time. Jackson was unanimously nominated by the Democratic National Party Convention meeting in Baltimore, Maryland. The National Republican Party, meeting in the same city, chose Henry Clay as its candidate. The rechartering of the Second Bank became the main campaign issue in the election. Jackson won a decisive victory, demonstrating that he was still popular with the majority of the people.

▲ *Still revered as a military hero, Jackson's popularity swept him into the presidency for a second term, in the election of 1832. This painting of him was done shortly thereafter.*

Second Administration, 1833–1837

On March 4, 1833, Jackson was inaugurated for his second term as president. Martin Van Buren, Jackson's secretary of state during his first administration, became vice president. The inauguration ceremony was peaceful and calm, in sharp contrast to Jackson's first inauguration. Jackson was too ill to attend the inaugural ball, but he had good cause to celebrate. Just two days earlier, South Carolina had finally agreed to the Compromise Tariff plan. The Union would survive, and Jackson could take the credit. Jackson soon embarked on a triumphal tour, traveling as far north as Concord, New Hampshire. Enthusiastic crowds greeted him at each stop, thrilled to catch a glimpse of the man who had saved the Union.

▶ Jackson Looks to End Second Bank

A thoroughly exhausted Jackson returned to Washington where he once again plunged into the battle against the Second Bank of the United States. Unless it was renewed, the Second Bank's charter would expire in 1836. Henry Clay and John C. Calhoun were organizing support in Congress on behalf of the bank. During the summer of 1833, Jackson told his cabinet that he planned to withdraw $11 million in federal funds, beginning on October 1, to hasten the bank's demise. When Secretary of the Treasury William J. Duane refused to carry out Jackson's instructions, Jackson replaced him with a new treasurer, Roger B. Taney.

Jackson distributed the federal funds from the Second Bank among various state banks. In retaliation, and in an attempt to pressure Jackson, the Second Bank refused to make loans, thereby threatening to derail the economy. As businesses failed and people lost their jobs, fear spread through the country. Many in Congress demanded that Jackson recharter the bank. Jackson, however, had the support of the people, who blamed the bank and not Jackson for the financial mess. Ultimately the Second Bank lost the battle when Congress, in April 1834, sustained Jackson's veto of the rechartering of the bank. In all, Jackson vetoed a dozen pieces of legislation—more than the combined number of vetoes by all former U.S. presidents.

The Specie Circular

In contrast to the conservative lending policies of the Second Bank, state banks extended easy credit—too easy, in fact. The flood of paper money led to excessive land speculation, especially in the West, and to inflation. In 1836, Jackson issued the Specie Circular, which required buyers of public lands to pay in gold or silver. (*Specie* is another word for "coins.") This put an end to land speculation, but it also dried up credit. The Specie Circular eventually led to a serious financial panic. This did not occur, however, until shortly after Jackson left office, in 1837.

Attempt on His Life

On January 30, 1835, Jackson had another close call with death, the latest in a long life filled with close calls. As Jackson was leaving the U.S. Capitol building that day, he was approached by Richard Lawrence, a mentally disturbed house painter. Lawrence tried to fire a shot at Jackson from a distance of about thirteen feet, but the gunpowder failed to ignite. As Jackson lunged at Lawrence with his cane, the man pulled out a second gun and fired at point-blank range. Amazingly, this gun also misfired. And so Jackson survived an assassination attempt, the first such attempt against the life of a U.S. president.

In 1836, Texas won its independence from Mexico, as Jackson's old friend Sam Houston led American forces to a decisive victory over the Mexican army. Houston became president of the new Republic of Texas, and appealed to Jackson to admit Texas to the Union. Jackson, however, aware of the growing tension over the issue of slavery, offered only to recognize the young republic rather than to push for statehood.

In the presidential election of 1836, Jackson's good friend Vice President Martin Van Buren was elected president. Jackson looked forward to saying a final farewell to the White House and to the nation, and to returning to the Hermitage.

▲ On January 30, 1835, a man named Richard Lawrence fired two guns in an attempt to assassinate President Andrew Jackson as he left the U.S. Capitol. This 1835 painting depicts the scene of yet another instance in which Old Hickory eluded death.

Last Years at the Hermitage, 1837–1845

On the evening of March 3, 1837, Andrew Jackson drank a toast to the Republic of Texas. He hoped to live long enough to see Texas admitted to the Union. The next day, March 4, Jackson shared the platform with Martin Van Buren as the new president was inaugurated.

▶ Leaving Office

In his farewell address, Jackson summed up the main points of his concept of democracy. He reminded the nation of the corrupting influence of money and said that liberty would survive only when defended by the uncorrupted. Sovereignty in America rested with the people. "To you," he told the American people, "everyone placed in authority is ultimately responsible. It is always in your power to see that the wishes of the people are carried into faithful execution, and their will, when once made known, must sooner or later be obeyed."[1] Jackson also warned of the growing bitterness between North and South over the issues of tariffs and slavery and cautioned Americans to preserve the Union at all costs.

Upon leaving the White House, Jackson took several weeks to make the long journey back to Tennessee. He stopped to visit old friends along the way. At every stop, Jackson was welcomed by large crowds of admirers.

▶ Retired Life

At the Hermitage, Jackson settled into a life of quiet retirement, which he had long been looking forward to. His daily routine included riding his horses and overseeing his cotton fields. Often he would entertain visitors. He maintained a keen interest in the political affairs of the day and often expressed his views in his letters to friends and key political figures.

Jackson was still interested in Texas. In 1844, when Sam Houston wrote him that if the U.S. government did not annex Texas, the republic would be forced to consider an alliance with Britain, Old Hickory was roused to action. He dashed off letters to U.S. senators, urging support for the annexation of Texas. He also gave his wholehearted support to James Polk in the presidential campaign that year, because Polk had spoken out in favor of annexation. Jackson was afraid that Henry Clay, Polk's opponent, would avoid taking a stand on Texas annexation. He was happy that Polk won the election.

Jackson Pushes for Texas Annexation

Polk was certainly not the only one in favor of annexing Texas. John Tyler, the retiring president, was also in favor. Even Jackson's old enemy from South Carolina, John C. Calhoun, supported annexation. Calhoun drafted a treaty of annexation, but could not get the necessary two-thirds vote in the Senate to ratify the treaty. Many senators would not go along with the treaty because they opposed adding another slave state to the Union. The annexation treaty was finally passed without the two-thirds majority. The two houses of Congress annexed Texas by a joint resolution, which required only a majority vote.

Before the Texas annexation could be finalized, Texas had to accept the treaty. Jackson became worried that perhaps Sam Houston's pride had been hurt by the reluctance of many in Congress to annex Texas and feared that

Houston would reject the treaty. Jackson wrote to his old friend, congratulating him and congratulating Texas. Still, no word came. Finally, on May 26, 1845, Jackson received a letter from Sam Houston confirming that Texas would indeed ratify the Treaty of Annexation.

▶ Jackson's Last Days

Jackson was greatly relieved. Now he could die in peace. On June 8, 1845, surrounded by family members and friends, Andrew Jackson, seventy-eight years of age, died. His last words were these: "Oh, do not cry. Be good children and we shall all meet in heaven."[2] About an hour later, a carriage pulled by galloping horses arrived at the Hermitage. Sam Houston burst into the room, accompanied by his young son. Tears came to his eyes when he realized he was too late to tell his old friend in person the good news about Texas.

▲ *After having served his country for more than 40 years, Andrew Jackson retired to his beloved Hermitage after leaving the presidency. This photograph shows the mansion as it looks today.*

Many historians regard Jackson as one of America's greatest presidents. He is considered the first truly modern president in that he believed he was elected to represent all the people, though he accepted slavery and refused to recognize the rights of American Indians. Jackson, not afraid to stand up to the wealthy and powerful, was the first American president to achieve the American dream of rising above a childhood steeped in poverty to become wealthy and powerful himself.

Chapter Notes

Chapter 1. Code of Honor

1. Margaret L. Coit, *Andrew Jackson* (Cambridge, Mass.: The Riverside Press, 1965), p. 7.

2. Burke Davis, *Old Hickory: A Life of Andrew Jackson* (New York: The Dial Press, 1977), p. 7.

3. Ibid., p. 49.

4. Ibid.

Chapter 2. Early Years, 1767–1788

1. Margaret L. Coit, *Andrew Jackson* (Cambridge, Mass.: The Riverside Press, 1965), p. 3.

Chapter 3. Frontier Hero, 1788–1828

1. Burke Davis, *Old Hickory: A Life of Andrew Jackson* (New York: The Dial Press, 1977), p. 18.

2. Margaret L. Coit, *Andrew Jackson* (Cambridge, Mass.: The Riverside Press, 1965), p. 72.

3. Davis, p. 195.

Chapter 4. First Administration, 1829–1833

1. Burke Davis, *Old Hickory: A Life of Andrew Jackson* (New York: The Dial Press, 1977), p. 251.

2. Howard Zinn, *A People's History of the United States: 1492–Present* (New York: HarperPerennial, 1995), p. 138.

3. Ibid., p. 139.

Chapter 6. Last Years at the Hermitage, 1837–1845

1. Robert V. Remini, *Andrew Jackson and the Course of American Democracy, 1833–1845* (New York: Harper & Row Publishers, 1984), vol. 3, p. 417.

2. Margaret L. Coit, *Andrew Jackson* (Cambridge, Mass.: The Riverside Press, 1965), p. 148.

Further Reading

Coit, Margaret L. *Andrew Jackson*. Cambridge, Mass.: The Riverside Press, 1965.

Davis, Burke. *Old Hickory: A Life of Andrew Jackson*. New York: The Dial Press, 1977.

James, Marquis. *Andrew Jackson: The Border Captain*. New York: Grosset & Dunlap, 1933.

———. *Andrew Jackson: Portrait of a President*. New York: Grosset & Dunlap, 1937.

Judson, Karen. *Andrew Jackson*. Springfield, N.J.: Enslow Publishers, Inc., 1997.

Osinski, Alice. *Andrew Jackson: Seventh President of the United States*. Chicago: Children's Press, 1987.

Remini, Robert V. *The Life of Andrew Jackson*. New York: Harper & Row Publishers, 1988.

Schlesinger, Arthur M., Jr. *The Age of Jackson*. Boston: Little, Brown & Company, 1953.

Sherrow, Victoria. *Cherokee Nation v. Georgia: Native American Rights*. Springfield, N.J.: Enslow Publishers, Inc., 1997.